T0413613

THE WORLD OF OCEAN ANIMALS
WALRUSES

by Mari Schuh

pogo

Ideas for Parents and Teachers

Pogo Books let children practice reading informational text while introducing them to nonfiction features such as headings, labels, sidebars, maps, and diagrams, as well as a table of contents, glossary, and index.

Carefully leveled text with a strong photo match offers early fluent readers the support they need to succeed.

Before Reading

- "Walk" through the book and point out the various nonfiction features. Ask the student what purpose each feature serves.
- Look at the glossary together. Read and discuss the words.

Read the Book

- Have the child read the book independently.
- Invite him or her to list questions that arise from reading.

After Reading

- Discuss the child's questions. Talk about how he or she might find answers to those questions.
- Prompt the child to think more. Ask: What did you know about walruses before reading this book? What more would you like to learn?

Pogo Books are published by Jump!
5357 Penn Avenue South
Minneapolis, MN 55419
www.jumplibrary.com

Library of Congress Cataloging-in-Publication Data

Names: Schuh, Mari C., 1975- author.
Title: Walruses / by Mari Schuh.
Description: Minneapolis, MN: Jump!, Inc., [2022]
Series: The world of ocean animals
Includes index. | Audience: Ages 7-10
Identifiers: LCCN 2021004087 (print)
LCCN 2021004088 (ebook)
ISBN 9781636900759 (hardcover)
ISBN 9781636900766 (paperback)
ISBN 9781636900773 (ebook)
Subjects: LCSH: Walrus–Juvenile literature.
Classification: LCC QL737.P62 S39 2022 (print)
LCC QL737.P62 (ebook) | DDC 599.79/9–dc23
LC record available at https://lccn.loc.gov/2021004087
LC ebook record available at https://lccn.loc.gov/2021004088

Editor: Jenna Gleisner
Designer: Michelle Sonnek

Photo Credits: Mikhail Cheremkin/Shutterstock, cover; Vladimir Melnik/Shutterstock, 1, 17; Vaclav Sebek/Shutterstock, 3, 16; blickwinkel/Alamy, 4; Menno Schaefer/Shutterstock, 5; juniors@wildlife Bildagentur G/Juniors/SuperStock, 6-7, 18-19; Theo Allofs/Minden Pictures/SuperStock, 8-9; Paul Souders/Getty, 10, 12-13; Nature Picture Library/Alamy, 11; zcw/Shutterstock, 12; Arterra Picture Library/Alamy, 14-15; PAUL BRADLEY/Alamy, 20-21; Inge Jansen/Shutterstock, 23.

Printed in the United States of America at Corporate Graphics in North Mankato, Minnesota.

TABLE OF CONTENTS

CHAPTER 1

STRONG TUSKS

A **herd** of walruses swims in the Arctic. They spend most of their lives in shallow, icy water.

tusk ·····▶

When it's time for a rest, walruses climb out. They use their strong tusks to pull themselves onto ice. They rest on ice and on land.

Tusks are useful in other ways, too. Walruses use them to make breathing holes in the ice. They also use them to fight. Males fight one another to show which is stronger. Two may fight over a **mate**.

DID YOU KNOW?

Walruses are very big. They do not have many **predators**. But orcas and polar bears sometimes hunt them. When this happens, walruses use their tusks to fight them.

When ice melts in the spring, some walruses **migrate** north. They look for thick ice. Why? Walruses are heavy. They can weigh more than 3,000 pounds (1,360 kilograms)! Ice has to be strong enough to hold them.

TAKE A LOOK!

Where do walruses live? Take a look!

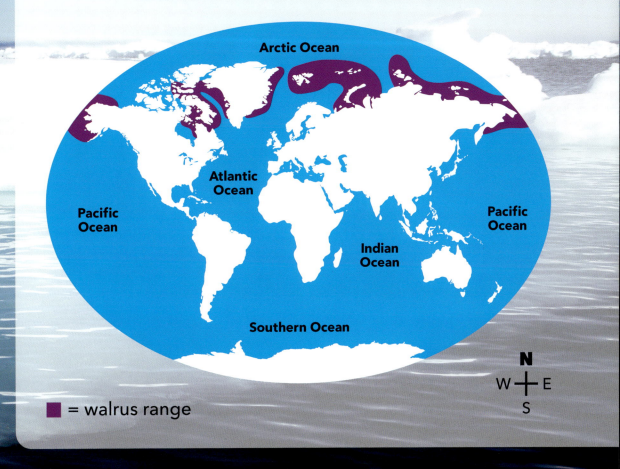

Arctic Ocean

Atlantic Ocean

Pacific Ocean

Pacific Ocean

Indian Ocean

Southern Ocean

N
W E
S

■ = walrus range

CHAPTER 2

SURVIVING IN THE ARCTIC

How do walruses stay safe in the Arctic? Thick, rough skin protects them during fights. **Blubber** keeps them warm. Large, flat flippers help them move on slippery ice.

flipper

In the water, flippers help walruses swim and **steer**. Walruses can stay underwater for up to 10 minutes.

Walruses dive to the ocean floor to find food. Their long whiskers feel for **prey** in the rocks and mud. Their noses dig out mussels and clams. Hungry walruses can eat more than 3,000 clams in one meal! Their tongues pull the shells apart. Then they suck the food out of the shells.

clams

whiskers

Walruses come to the surface to breathe. They have air sacs under their throats. These fill with air. This helps walruses float. When they sleep in the water, their heads stay above the surface.

TAKE A LOOK!

What are a walrus's body parts called? Take a look!

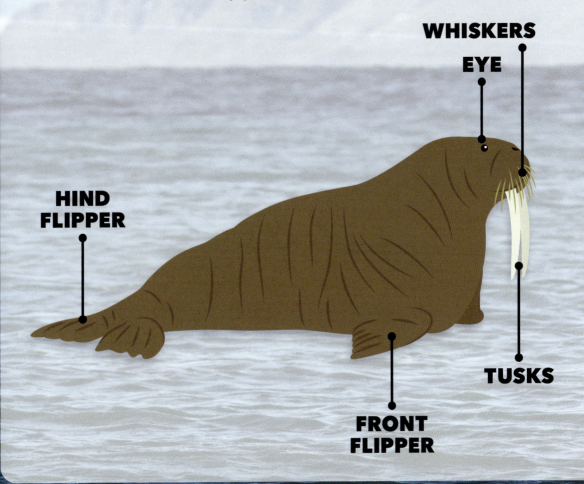

WHISKERS

EYE

HIND FLIPPER

TUSKS

FRONT FLIPPER

CHAPTER 3

WALRUS HERDS

Walruses are noisy. They make sounds in the water and on land. They whistle, click, and tap. They also roar and cough. Why? This is how they **communicate**.

Walruses are very **social**. They live together in herds. Some herds are small. Others can have around 40,000 walruses! Males and females live in separate herds.

calf

Walruses are **mammals**. A female gives birth to live young. She has one **calf** at a time. A calf weighs about 130 pounds (59 kg) at birth. It drinks its mother's milk as it grows. The mother keeps her calf close to protect it.

Mothers teach their calves how to swim. At just one month old, calves are strong swimmers. But they still sometimes catch a ride on their moms' backs!

Female calves often stay with their mothers. Male calves join herds of male walruses. They all grow up in the icy Arctic water.

DID YOU KNOW?

Climate change is melting Arctic ice. This means less space for walruses to rest and care for their young. How can you help walruses?

ACTIVITIES & TOOLS

SOUNDS IN WATER

Walruses make sounds both in and out of the water. Learn which sounds are louder with this activity.

What You Need:
- two drinking glasses
- water
- butter knife

1 Fill one glass full of warm water. Keep the other glass empty.

2 Carefully place your ear inside the empty drinking glass. Gently tap the side of the glass with the butter knife. Listen to the sound it makes. How loud is it?

3 Now carefully place your ear inside the glass with water. Have an adult help you.

4 Gently tap the side of the glass with the butter knife. Listen to the sound it makes. Is the sound louder this time?

Water is more dense than air. This means sound waves travel faster in water. This makes the sound louder.

GLOSSARY

blubber: A thick layer of fat under the skin of some ocean animals.

calf: A young walrus.

climate change: Changes in Earth's weather and climate over time.

communicate: To share information, ideas, or feelings with another.

herd: A group of walruses.

mammals: Warm-blooded animals that give birth to live young, which drink milk from their mothers.

mate: The male or female partner of a pair of animals.

migrate: To travel from one place to another place during different times of the year.

predators: Animals that hunt other animals for food.

prey: Animals that are hunted by other animals for food.

social: Living in groups rather than on their own.

steer: To make something move in a particular direction.

INDEX

TO LEARN MORE

Finding more information is as easy as 1, 2, 3.

❶ Go to www.factsurfer.com

❷ Enter "walruses" into the search box.

❸ Choose your book to see a list of websites.

FACT SURFER